52 Weeks
52 Dates

"I WILL NEVER STOP TRYING. BECAUSE WHEN YOU FIND
THE ONE...
YOU NEVER GIVE UP."

—CRAZY, STUPID, LOVE

VON WEIKI

A PERSONAL LETTER FROM US,

We used to have relationship problems too, but one day we decided
to change something about it.
We started to take turns planning a date every week
for each other.

Since then, our relationship is exactly how we always wanted it to be.
It is varied and balanced.

That's why we decided to help others who may be in the same
situation as we were then, with a collection of dates carefully selected.

Positive reviews from wonderful people like you will help other couples feel confident in choosing our date book. That's why we'd love it
if you take two minutes to review our book on Amazon.

We would be happy if you share your experiences with us!

Have a lot of fun with the book 52 Weeks - 52 Dates!

FOREWORD

Everyday life can be tough, filled with many obligations. Kids, work, household ... a seemingly endless list. In all the chaos, we often lose sight of the most important thing:
our love

Thereby, it's so important to make time for each other, because otherwise love, that special tingle in your stomach, will slowly fade away. A great way to keep romantic feelings alive is through
unique dates

We found that one date per week is a good rhythm.
So here are 52 dates for 52 weeks.

Enjoy the inspiration for great dates and your time together!

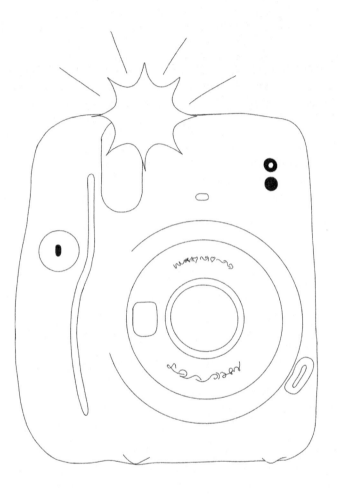

MEMORIES ARE FOREVER

Pictures stay with us forever and remind us of the beautiful moments we have experienced.

That's why we recommend:
Buy a Polaroid camera, which you can get on Amazon for very little money.

Take one picture per date and write in the white field below the picture what you did and the date. So the memory can remain forever.
At the end of the book you will find three creative ideas what you can do with the Polaroid photos.

Scan this code for the most popular Polaroid camera!

☐ 1. Go for a hike or a walk in nature

Whether you're in the countryside or in a big city, discover the great outdoors together.

Pick a hike that fits your fitness level, and pack something to drink and some snacks.

City people: Explore the parks in your city or look for hiking trails near the city.

☐ 2. Join a yoga lesson together

Time to test your flexibility!
Challenge it during a yoga class together.

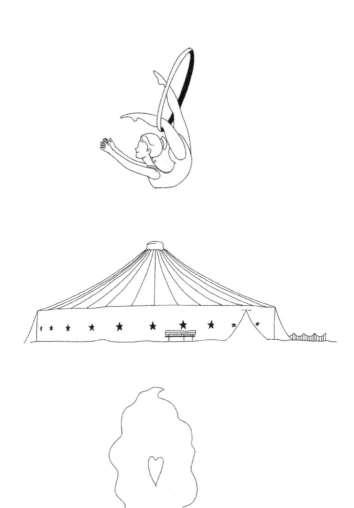

☐ 3. Visits a fair, circus or carnival

Sweets, carousels and fantastic shows.
Animal friendly: Acrobat Shows!

☐ 4.Book a cooking or baking lesson

Cooking is fun! Especially together.

Budget-friendly option: No need for a chef to show you what to do. Just pick a delicious recipe, buy the ingredients and stick to the recipe. Youtube is very helpful for this.

☐ 5. Take a ride in a hot air balloon

We recommend a hot air balloon ride for special occasions, such as a special birthday or anniversary. It will be an unforgettable moment to cheer with a glass of Prosecco far above the ground and between the clouds.

☐ 6. Get drunk together at a wine or beer tasting.

Test your taste buds and try not to get drunk too quickly. If you prefer something with more oomph, try a whiskey, gin or liquor tasting.

Non-drinkers: don't worry, there's plenty more to try than just alcohol. From antipasti to cheesecakes, you're sure to find the right tasting.

☐ 7. Take a dance class

Dancing is sexy. Even if you don't know a single step yet, learning is a lot of fun.

And who knows, maybe there will be a wedding soon where your dancing skills will be used ;)

8. Visit a nearby beach or lake

Packing List:
- Towels, blankets or chairs
- Cooler with soft drinks, beer, ice
- Sunscreen or umbrella
- Water polo and other fun games
- Snacks and more snacks

☐ 9. Go to a museum or art gallery

"Art is in the eye of the beholder"
Let yourself be surprised what kind of art you like or don't
like. Maybe you will even find inspiration for the walls in
home.

☐ 10. Go to a sports event

Go to the stadium and watch a game live. The feeling of
being there in person is guaranteed to surpass the broadcasts
on television. Even if you don't follow sports yet, it's worth
watching a sporting event live. Depending on the season,
football, ice hockey or tennis is a good choice.

☐ 11. Take a boat trip

Whether it's a fast motorboat, a big steamer or a cozy pedal boat, being out on the water is fun!

☐ 12. Visit an aquarium or a zoo

Very cute meerkats, big sharks or lazy pandas, there is always something to see at the zoo.

Advice: Inquire best about the feeding times, this is usually very spectacular.

☐ 13. Have fun at a concert or festival

Music touches us deep in the heart, even more so when we experience it live. Surprise your partner with tickets to his or her favorite band.

☐ 14. Winter date: skiing or snowboarding

Often smaller ski resorts are cheaper than the big popular ones and also less visited, which meansmore space on the ropes! Afterwards you can warm up with a spiced up tea or Jägermeister.

ADVICE:

Many of the date ideas can also be arranged as a double date with one or more couples. It is important that you spend time with just the two of you, but it can be fun to invite another couple.

In addition, the exchange with other couples is important and can be very helpful.

1. It renews the relationship.
When you've been in a relationship for a long time, it can be easy to fall into a routine and make things a little monotonous. A double date can help freshen up the relationship by getting to know each other in a different context and keeping things interesting.

2. Make new friends.
A double date can also be a great way to make new friends. It can be fun to spend time with other couples and get to know each other.

3. Support and advice from other couples.
A double date can also be a good way to get support and advice from other couples. When you are in a long-term relationship, it can be difficult to get perspective, and it can be helpful to learn from other couples who may have been together for longer and have had similar experiences.

☐ 15. Go to an indoor trampolin park or an indoor climbing place

Jumping on a trampoline is still a lot of fun in adulthood. Have you ever heard of jumping warriors or ninja warriors? Many indoor parks offer obsticle trails similar to those on TV. Try how far and fast you can get.

☐ 16. Laugh till you drop from your chairs in a comedy show

Laughing together until your abs hurt is something that connects. From big comedy shows to small stand up performances.

☐ 17. Visit a theme park or water park

Disneyland, Universal Studios or Harry Potter World are not just fun for kids. There are also plenty of cool attractions, rides, fan moments and more for adults as well.

☐ 18. Take a riding lesson or trail ride together

Even if you have never been on a horse before, you can book trail rides in the surrounding countryside at many horse farms. If you don't yet dare to go into the open countryside, try how it feels to sit on a horse in a riding lesson beforehand.

☐ 19. Take a cinematic landscape drive

Whether on two or four wheels: with your own car, motorcycle or a (rental) convertible, a drive through the countryside is especially beautiful in spring, summer or autumn.

Tip: For a nice ending, pick a cozy inn at the end of the ride.

☐ 20. Watch a ballet or go to the theater

Dress up fancy and enjoy a performance at the ballet or theater. During the break maybe have a nice a glass of champagne?

☐ 21. Play bowling against each other

Get into your bowling shoes and let's go! A bowling date is a true classic and therefore often appears in Hollywood movies.

□ 22. Take a pottery or painting class together

It's great to let off steam creatively, and who knows, maybe there's an artist in one of you? In any case, you will have created new works of art for your home.

Budget-friendly option: get two canvases, some paints and just paint away. If you want more structure, you can also watch painting tutorials on YouTube, such as Bob Ross.

☐ 23. Take part in a guided tour or a historical city walk

There are hidden stories in every town and especially as a resident you should know a little bit about the history of your own town.

If you live in a village and there are no guided tours, you can go to the nearest castle or open-air museum and learn about the surroundig history.

☐ 24. Try to solve an Escape-Room

This date is also perfect for a double date or invite some of your friends for a fun experience together.

☐ 25. Take part in a wine or brewery tour

It doesn't always have to be just a tasting. Often you can also see the whole brewery, whiskey distillery or winery. This way you learn exciting info about your favorite alcohol.

Sometimes you can find adventure breweries, such as the Heineken brewery in Amsterdam.

26. Stroll through a local botanical garden

A date does not always have to be elaborate and long. Sometimes it's also really nice to take a simple walk together and talk about whatever comes to mind.

Tip: You can make funny word games with the plant names.

☐ 27. Spend a day at a thermal bath or spa

There is hardly a more relaxed date!
Often there are also "offers for two", meaning couple packages with massages, double couches and complementary glass of prosecco.

☐ 28. Halloweendate: Haunted house or spooky tour

Okay, it doesn't have to be on Halloween exactly, a spooky
date is a guaranteed thrill all year round.

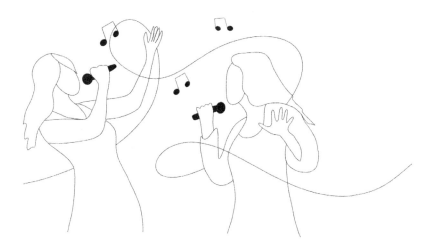

29. Sing in a karaoke bar

Whether you can sing or not, it's incredibly fun to sing!

Love songs are especially good for this, kind of like performing a musical "I love you".

30. Take a city tour by bike

If you don't have your own bike, you can rent one in most cities for a reasonable price. Sports stores also offer bikes for rent. Feel free to make stops and, for example, get a delicious ice cream for refreshment.

31. Shop fresh ingredients at a farmers market and cook a delicious meal

Stroll through the market, taste what's on offer and create a great meal at home with the fresh ingredients.
For inspiration ask the farmers what they like to cook with their produce.

☐ 32. Go to a skateboard or BMX track

If that's a little too daring for you, we recommend trying longboards. Riding a longboard is not only fun, but also easier to learn. In addition to the large wheels, the width of the axles also makes for safer riding.

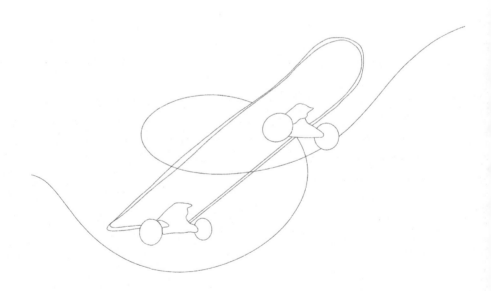

☐ 33. Go to a local bookstore and buy a book for the other

Who doesn't know it, you come home and are tired, turn up the TV and watch a show until you fall asleep?
An evening of reading together is a great way to change up this routine. It is so cozy to sit next to each other on the couch and read a good book.

Go to a bookstore and pick great books together or for each other.

☐ 34. Take a trip by canoe or kayak

At many lakes there are offers to borrow a canoe or kayak and it's worth it. The surrounding landscapes can be admired incredibly well from the lake and it is a perfect photo spot.

THE 10 MOST IMPORTANT FACTORS FOR A HEALTHY AND HAPPY RELATIONSHIP:

1. Communication:
Good communication is the key to a good relationship. It is important to speak openly and honestly with each other and to listen to each other.

2. Trust:
Trust is an important foundation for any relationship. It is essential that both partners trust each other fully and trust that the other respects their needs and feelings. That brings us to the next point.

3. Respect:
Respect is crucial to maintaining a happy and healthy relationship. It is important that both partners see and regard each other as equals.

4. Understanding:
In a good partnership, both partners must try to understand the perspective and feelings of the other. This requires empathy and the ability to put oneself in the other's shoes.

5. Teamwork:
In a relationship, both partners work together to reach common goals and overcome challenges. They support and encourage each other and share responsibility for the well-being of the relationship.

6. Support:
In a healthy relationship, there is mutual support and caring. Both partners are there to stand by each other in difficult times and to care for each other.

7. Equality:

In any relationship, both partners are equal and have the same rights and responsibilities. There is no power imbalance or dominance of one partner over the other.

8. Freedom:

In a healthy partnership, there is enough freedom for each partner to pursue their own interests and hobbies and to have time to themselves.

9. Satisfaction:

In a happy relationship, both partners are satisfied and happy. They feel respected and valued and that their needs and desires are met.

10. Solve conflicts together:

Every relationship has disagreements or arguments from time to time, and it is important that both partners learn how to resolve these conflicts in a productive way.

This includes listening to each other, giving constructive feedback, and finding solutions that are acceptable to both parties. It is also important to make an effort to understand the other person's feelings and perspective and not be fixated only on your own needs.

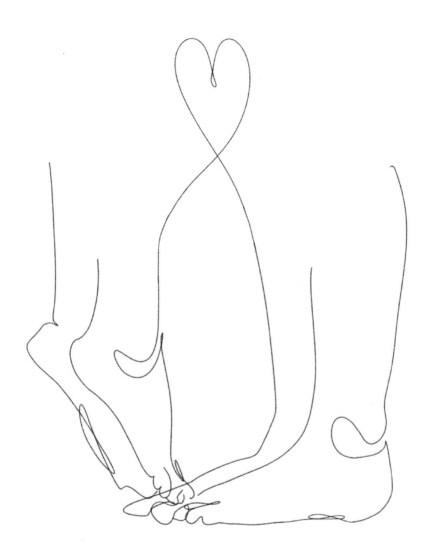

☐ 35. Ice skating: The perfect winterdate!

Get into your warm winter jackets and get on the ice. Hold on to each other until you are safe on your skates and if you get cold we recommended to get a tea and mulled wine.

☐ 36. Get a pedicure together

Your feet will thank you, whether one of you is already a regular pedicurist or you've never been before. Sitting next to each other and gossiping while your feet are being done is incredibly fun.

☐ 37. Roller skating in funky outfits

Rollerskating in sporty 80s or 90s outfit. The outfits will not only put you in a good mood, but will automatically turn you into roller skating pros. If you still need inspiration for your outfits, we recommend the series "Stranger Things" and music videos from the 1980s on Youtube.

☐ 38. Treat yourselfs to a couple massage

Who doesn't need a little relaxing time out? Whether it's a foot massage, Thai massage or hot stone. Massages are soothing and relaxing.

Budget-friendly option: There are great massage instructions on YouTube. Light some candles at home, prepare some body lotion or oil and take turns massaging each other.

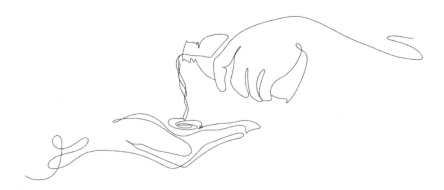

☐ 39. Try a new cuisine or go to a new restaurant

Dinner dates are a popular classic among dates. However, your task here is to discover a new cuisine. Have you ever eaten Persian or Korean food? Try it.

40. Go to the cinema and let a stranger decide which movie you watch

It can be a funny situation if you ask strangers which movie you should watch. Another option would be to ask your friends and let them choose the movie for you.

Have a good time while you're at it. Big popcorn? Well, of course!
Nachos are not to be missed and as much candy as you want.

☐ 41. Buy something exciting in a sex shop

Choose a new toy or accessories together, have fun ;)

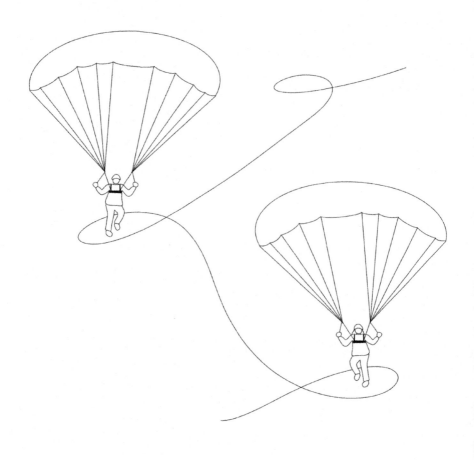

☐ 42. Take a ride with paraglider

This will be a super exciting date. You two will float over the world and look at everything from above. This will remain in your memories forever.

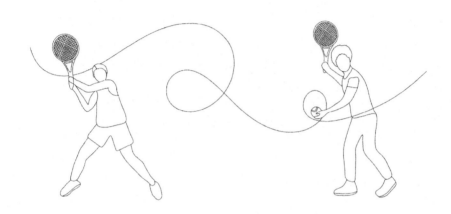

43. Play tennis or squash together

It's high time to try tennis if you never played before because even without much previous knowledge, it's fun.

For squash, a ball is played by two players alternately against one or more walls. The goal is to play the ball in such a way that the opponent does not reach the ball before it touches the ground for the second time.

Tip: This point is very suitable for a double date.

44. Dinner in the Dark

Dinner without any light! Not even a single candle. Yes, and it's really exciting and fun to rely completely on other senses.

Important: Wear clothes that can get dirty.

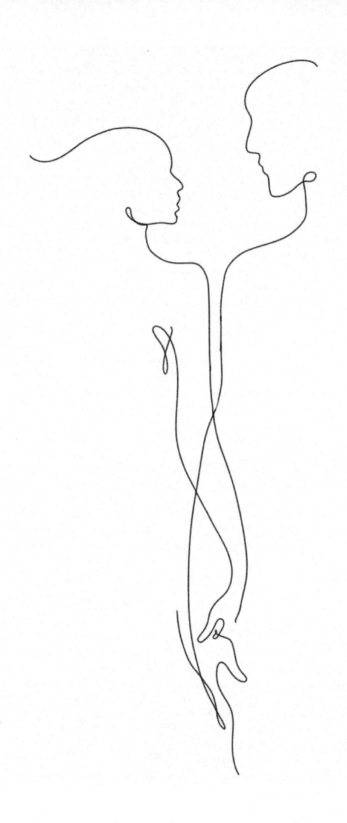

☐ 45. Discover your city or village anew with Atlas Obscura

Atlas Obscura is a different kind of travel guide. It doesn't suggest the beautiful, classic and well-known sights, but the weird and absurd things to discover in your city.

Just google Atlas Obscura + the name of your city.

☐ 46. Immerse yourself in the gourmet cuisine and book a multi-course menu

Edible art, is probably the best description for the creations from the gourmet food. Depending on your budget, you'll find restaurants ranging from one to five toques. Even without a toque, restaurants often offer fantastic multi-course menus.

☐ 47. Photoshooting

Book a photoshoot and take great pictures that you can hang up in your home and/or post on your social media channels. Such high-quality pictures are always amazing to look at.

Budget-friendly option: Ask your friends if they have a camera and would like to do a photoshoot with you. Or if you can borrow the camera and a tripod to take your own photos.

☐ 48. Try your luck in a casino

Blackjack, roulette or poker? Just roll the dice! Who knows, maybe you'll go home with a big win?

49. Float in a Floating Tank

Something completely new for the senses. In the floating tank you float in 35°C warm salt water in complete silence and darkness. As a couple you are together in a large tank.

For many people floating is very calming, for some it stimulates creativity and some even report something similar to psychedelic visions.

☐ 50. Book a hotel room in your city.

 You don't always have to go far to take a vacation and book a hotel. Surprise your partner with a nice hotel room in your city or in a nearby city and view the whole thing like a vacation that lasts one night.

Leaving your own four walls provides excitement and tingling.

51. Visit an observatory or planetarium.

There is hardly anything more romantic than looking up at the stars together. Since this is often difficult, especially in cities or villages due to light pollution, it is a good idea to go to a planetarium or observatory.

☐ 52. Giving love back

Just as beautiful as receiving love is giving love.

Spend a day together helping out at an animal shelter, soup kitchen or charity of your choice.

Polaroid fairy lights

Polaroid Holder

3 CREATIVE IDEAS
FOR YOUR PICTURES

1. Clothespins:
Use clothespins to hang the Polaroids from a string strung from the ceiling or along a wall. This creates a fun and casual arrangement that can be easily rearranged.
There are also already Polaroid light strings, so the memories are also always well lit.
Simply scan the QR code on the left.

2. Polaroid holder:
Buy these cute Polaroid stands. Use them to show off your favorite photos on a table or shelf. Keep the rest of your Polaroids. That way you can keep switching through and showing off all your adventures in turn.

3. Photowall:
Create a photo wall by arranging the Polaroids in a grid or unique arrangement on a large blank wall. This can be with small pins on a cork wall or with glue dots on the wall itself.

THANK YOU

Weiki would like to thank you for purchasing this book.

We really hope you enjoyed trying out the dates.

Positive reviews from
wonderful people like you will help other couples feel confident in
choosing our date book. That's why we'd love it if you took two minutes to review our book on Amazon.

All the love!

Printed in Great Britain
by Amazon